KUNDALINI,

AN OCCULT
EXPERIENCE

G. S. Arundale

Published 2014; 2016
Copyright © 2016 Aziloth Books

British Library Cataloguing in Publication Data

A catalogue record for this book is available from the British Library

ISBN-13: 978-1-911405-00-9

Printed and bound in Great Britain by Lightning Source UK Ltd., 6 Precedent Drive, Rooksley, Milton Keynes MK13 8PR.

Cover Illustration: *Hindu Chakra Painting.*
Anonymous (19th Century)

TABLE OF CONTENTS

This book is emphatically not a guide to the awakening of Kundalini. On the other hand, there is an aura encircling all rightful experiments and experiences, which can be conveyed even through the medium of print. This aura not only clears the outlook of the earnest student of life, but also helps to raise his consciousness to the more rarefied levels where the Eternal dwells less veiled by the shadows of time.

Glimpses of Kundalini in action are vouchsafed the student who is content to watch and not to grasp. Let the descriptions be read lightly, not with the mind but with the intuition. Thus, however fantastic they may seem, yet the reader will perceive that they are fantastic not because they are untrue but because they are too true.

Is there a Kundalini chain linking the constituent elements of our own solar system, and another chain linking together the various solar systems? Surely so, and speculation is no less interesting as to the nature of the centres of a solar system and as to their vivification by Cosmic Kundalini. To understand this tremendous vista it is necessary to learn how to arouse and direct Kundalini to the various centres of the vehicles of a human being.

CHAPTER 3. THE DANGERS OF KUNDALINI

Can the brain stand the pressure? This and the sex danger are, perhaps, the principal questions with regard to the arousing of Kundalini. Extreme circumspection is vital, for the Serpent-Fire does not discriminate. It consumes. It tends to flow along the lines of least resistance, and sometimes such lines may lead downwards and not upwards, with indescribably disastrous effect.

CHAPTER 4. KUNDALINI ACTIVE EVERYWHERE

Wherever there is life, there is Kundalini more or less awake and awakening. But the conscious direction and handling of its power is another matter altogether. One of the effects of Kundalini is the intensification of the sense of Unity. A breaker-down of barriers between the various layers and states of consciousness, Kundalini is also the breaker of barriers between the individual himself and the larger Self without.

CHAPTER 5. THE DEVELOPMENT OF KUNDALINI

In the beginnings of this process dizziness is noticeable, which is perhaps the physical expression of a new relativity, of a new adjustment, other worlds than the physical beginning to be open to a gaze which the individual has not yet learned to control. Sensitiveness is enormously increased, making the individual a kind of sensitive plate upon which, for example, people in the outer world imprint themselves, so that in a flash he knows their natures, especially the high lights of quality and the low lights of defect.

The heart of the earth is one pole of Kundalini, the Sun is the other. Now the awakening of Kundalini is tantamount to making oneself the Rod between the two. In one sense one ever is a Rod, but the Rod is not yet alive, awake. It is asleep or dreaming, and the Fire itself slumbers. To awaken Kundalini is to fan the Fire into a consuming flame, burning, purifying, energizing, making conscious contact with the Universal Fire.

Whether in fact clairvoyance, etc., arises or not, though in course of time it will, is of far less importance than the definite establishment of the higher consciousness - Buddhic and later Nirvanic - in the waking consciousness, which is the high purpose of the arousing of Kundalini. This means an extraordinary vivification of Intuition - pure knowledge undistorted by the personal equation. One even feels inclined to tell some of one's friends, if they ask, quite frankly what they need.

It seems as if Kundalini can be sent forth from any centre though preferably from the solar plexus centre or from the centre between the eyebrows. We thus begin to realize that the great centres of the body are the main distributors of force. It is not a matter of eyes or hands or feet, but of centres.

In some mysterious way Kundalini remains for ever individual to its recipient, however much it may always be inseparable from the Universal Fire whence it issues forth. In some mysterious way it partakes of the nature of the Permanent Atom, cannot disintegrate, and forms the eternal Fire of the evolving individuality.

Kundalini is music as well as colour. It is a throbbing majesty of sound and a rainbow of colour, Kundalini sings with the voice of all that lives. In the singing is heard the voice of the Unity of Life, and in the colours is felt the Warmth of Life.

The student finds himself on a stream of Kundalini, and moves on the stream towards time's beginnings so far as this particular evolution is concerned. He moves back and back and back, until he finds himself strangely immersed in the majestic profundities of the opening of a new era of life.

EXPLANATION

In this brief account of a number of experiments and experiences with Kundalini, called the Serpent-Fire for its seemingly tortuous movements and its triple power of creating, preserving and destroying-regenerating - a veritable trinity of activity within a mighty stream of life - I have deliberately refrained from any comparison between statements contained in responsible Kundalini literature, scattered, few and veiled as these must necessarily be, and the conclusion to which the experiments and experiences seemed at the time to lead. I want these experiments and experiences to give their own atmosphere, uncorroborated and standing by themselves.

All statements regarding Kundalini should always be treated with the greatest reserve, partly because the personal equation of the experimenting individual looms very large - Kundalini acting very differently in different cases - and partly because nothing ought to appear in print which might give even the slightest assistance in the development of a power which destroys ruthlessly when it is sought to be awakened before its due time.

On the other hand, there is an aura encircling all rightful experiments and experiences which can be conveyed even through the medium of print; and I venture to think that this aura not only clears the outlook of the earnest student of life, but also helps to raise his consciousness to the more rarefied levels where the Eternal dwells less veiled by the fleeting, but nonetheless relatively impenetrable,shadows of time.

KUNDALINI AN OCCULT EXPERIENCE is emphatically not a guide to awakening the forces of Kundalini. That is for the individual and for those Elder Brethren whom he will sooner or later meet when he has outgrown the nursing of the ordinary everyday circumstances of the outer world. The outer world can help an individual up to a certain point. It may see him through his school career. But at last he begins to have learned the lessons the outer world can teach him, and thus becomes ready for life's more advanced courses in the inner worlds. Kundalini is a lesson in such inner worlds, part of the curriculum which prepares him for his Master's degree.

KUNDALINI AN OCCULT EXPERIENCE, an experience in the as yet little known field of the Serpent-Fire, is published far more for the sake of the mystery of the adventure than for the sake of any precise knowledge which may have been gained. Indeed, the book is not published for the sake of a knowledge of Kundalini, but for the sake of introducing its readers to the fact that Kundalini is a mystery, but an intriguing and fascinating mystery. All knowledge, for true understanding, must at first be a mystery as well as an experience. It should be approached softly and with bated breath, reverently, with joyous eagerness, and with the sense of being in the midst of a great beyond. All true knowledge is a mystery for ever and ever, for however much we may know, or think we know, there is always the wondrous more drawing us onwards and upwards, giving more beautiful worth to that which is already ours, and making our pathway to Divinity an ever-increasing delight.

I am hoping that the discerning reader will rest content with envelopment in provocative mystery, will be satisfied with what I hope will prove a comfortable stretching of his consciousness so that he hardly knows where he is, so that in his very waking consciousness he receives intimations of certain larger states, of peaks in those Himalayan heights, which await his conquering. It is sometimes good when one is in darkness to be reminded of the light which some day shall pierce it. Let the reader lose his time-imprisoned self in the mystery of Kundalini as he should be constantly losing this time-self in many another mystery. Thus losing himself he shall gradually learn himself to adventure forth into all mysteries, and at last to hear the Silver Voices chanting to him of his Ascension.

To dwell in knowledge is beautiful and helpful, but no less beautiful and helpful is it to dwell in mystery, for in mystery Gods learn to know themselves as God.

Let us first be flotsam of the depths, floating peacefully and safely on their calm and sheltering surfaces, ere we seek to penetrate their profundities against their righteously rebellious shatterings, designed not to protest but to test worthiness to seek. Let us know them face to face in peace, before we plunge into the storms and cataclysms which make us one with them.

I hope that a perusal of this little book will at least cause, in each understanding reader, an adjustment of his individual consciousness to a larger consciousness of which it is a part. Such adjustment should be in the nature of an expansion, a sense of happy stretching, of exhilaration, of a joyous ascent into the mountains of his being, of an exploration of himself such as he has probably not so far undertaken.

Finally, I apologize for all redundancies and obscure wordings. The redundancies were inevitable, since the experience sometimes repeated itself, and I have thought it better to leave the experience in its original form of translation into outer world language. The obscure wordings result from the endeavour to express that which to the student was inexpressible. These obscure wordings I have also left untouched.

G. S. A.

THE NATURE OF KUNDALINI

CHAPTER 1

What is Kundalini? The Samskrit word has been variously translated, generally by those who have no real conception whatever as to the function of that of which it is the label.

It seems that the root of the word is the verb *kund*, which signifies "to burn". This is the vital meaning, for Kundalini is Fire in its aspect of burning. But we have a further explanation of the word in the noun *kunda*, which means a hole or a bowl. Here we are given an idea of the vessel in which the Fire burns. But there is even more than this. There is also the noun *kundala*, which means a coil, a spiral, a ring. Here we are given an idea as to the way in which the Fire works, unfolds. Out of all these essential derivatives the word Kundalini is born, giving creative femininity to the Fire, Serpent-Fire as it is sometimes called, the feminine creative power asleep within a bowl, within a womb, awakening to rhythmic movement in up-rushing and downpouring streams of Fire. It is a word signifying the feminine aspect of the creative force of evolution, which force in its specialized and more individual potency lies asleep, curled up as in a womb, at the base of the human spine. Its awakening is fraught with the utmost danger, indeed disaster, save as the individual concerned is in a position to keep it under full control. And such power to control comes only when the higher reaches of the evolutionary way are being approached, reaches still out of sight as regards the vast majority of mankind.

Now and then, however, glimpses of Kundalini in action are vouchsafed to the student who is content to watch and not to grasp, and the following descriptions are of Kundalini at work before the eyes of such a student, he interpreting what he saw as best he could, often no doubt faultily. The experiences were interspersed with some authorized experiments, and while it is as impossible as it is unlawful for one student to share with any other his experiences and experiments in any degree of fullness, it being still more impossible and unlawful for any indication to be given as to the mode of awakening Kundalini - the mode varies substantially according to the soul-note of the individual - yet now and then is permitted a sharing of the atmosphere of these experiences and experiments, at least in some measure.

It is hoped that the result will be a subtle awakening of the larger consciousness, of the shadow of a shade of the spirit of Cosmic consciousness; so that there may arise a fragrance of what may be called spiritual ozone, in the exhilaration of which the reader contacts a self of his Self larger than any he has so far known within the limitations of his present incarnation. He achieves a release, a freedom. He becomes like a bird which has at last begun to find the use of his wings. He flutters, even if he cannot yet fly. And in that very fluttering he begins to distinguish between the real and the unreal, between the true and the false, between the useful and the useless, between the beautiful and the ugly. And though he remains unable constantly to use the discrimination thus aroused, at least he knows, he experiences, and sooner or later the knowledge-experience becomes steady activity. When it begins so to do, then is the time for those first feeble stirrings of Kundalini which shall eventually release in him for ever the Fire of Life and place upon him the Crown-Flower of eternal Kingship.

We all are far away from Kingship, but perhaps the experiences and experiments herein set forth may be intimations, however faint, of a fragment of the nature of royal living, and thus give courage to endure and courage to conquer.

I have not edited these experiences and experiments so as to make them intelligible, still less conventionally rational. I have left them just as they came, with only slight modifications. Their value does not lie in their appeal to the reason, but in their recognition as a reflection of something which the earnest student will know to be his as well. He will see in the very incomprehensibility of much that is described a something towards which he feels he too is irresistibly moving. However fantastic they may seem, yet somehow he perceives that they are fantastic not because they are untrue, but because they are still too true for him. I hope that when they may seem absurd he will feel that their absurdity lies only in their being so utterly foreign to all normal experience and experiment, not in their being nonsense. Even if they may appear nonsense to his limited sense, perhaps to some they may seem more sense, and his sense more non-sense.

Let the descriptions be read lightly, not with the mind but with the intuition, not with an already set conviction as to what can and what cannot be, but with the mind, the heart and the will open to all things. Let the reader be fully aware that the unbelievable is by no means necessarily untrue, and that the consciousness we call "I," with its various functionings - physical, emotional, mental and beyond - is infinitely more extraordinary than even our wildest dreams could envisage.

THE UNIVERSE-KUNDALINI
AND CENTRES

CHAPTER 2

The last sentence in the foregoing chapter brings us at once to the startling opening which heralded these various experiences and experiments.

In the first flash of intuitional and possibly higher expansion, the subject of the experiences became engulfed in a sense of the relationship between the microcosm and the macrocosm. He is, for the time, carried off his feet. His consciousness flashes outwards to what seems to be the furthest confines of space, and he becomes absorbed in the glorious and perfect certainty-giving fact of the intimate unity of his own consciousness, not only with the universal consciousness, in so far as the word " universal " may at all be rightly used when there seems to be a universal beyond the infinite, but also with specific parts of the universal consciousness. His own individual consciousness is a piece of mosaic in the pattern of evolving life, and there are other pieces seemingly closely linked to his as being of the same general rate of vibration, of the same colour. Where are there mosaics similar in general principle to his? And at once, as in response, vibrations seem to come from afar and from a very precise afar not here to be more defined. There is clearly an immense Cosmic significance of the twin-soul theory, might I not say the multiple-soul theory, by no means within the compass of this tiny little world of ours. And let it be said at once that the commonplace twin-soul idea current in certain phases of modern thought is a very poor caricature of a marvellous reality. This very earth has its twin-star, and it becomes clear at once that the duality of life is no less fundamental than its unity, or than its trinity. But further speculation is denied. It will not be profitable at this stage.

In the light of this special intuition the speculation also arises, as the student is carried still further off his feet, though not so wildly that there is no substance in his shadows, as to the relation between the great occult Rites of the Fire on this earth, and the Universe-Kundalini of which our Lord the Sun is the heart as well as the body. For us, the Sun is Kundalini *in excelsis*, in which we live and move and have our being. Each individual Kundalini in whatever kingdom of nature, in whatever substance - great or small - in whatever world, is part of the Sun-Kundalini. And, strange as it may seem, these tiny Kundalini streams partake of the omniscience, omnipotence, omnipresence, of their sublime Progenitor. Thus may we say that all life, each one of us, is omnipotent, omniscient, omnipresent, in the becoming. There is a most intimate connection between the Fire of our Lord the Sun and the universe-life which He has set afire.

It becomes clear at once that Kundalini, howsoever it may appear, is mighty and torrential, here mighty and torrential in potentiality only, there stirring and awakening, elsewhere in resistless movement, burning all before it.

Is there a Kundalini chain linking the constituent elements of our own solar system, and another chain linking the various solar systems? Surely so, and speculation is no less interesting as to the nature of the centres of a solar system and on their vivification by Cosmic Kundalini. The Earth has its centres - whirling wheels of fiery energy - and it would appear that one of the functions of some of the Lords of Evolution is the regulation of distribution and intensity of Kundalini. This is a reason why even Their work has been described as hazardous, like the work of those who bring ammunition to the front line trenches in time of war. They might in some way, perhaps, be consumed with the very Force They wield, though it may be supposed that in Their case this could not happen.

As a preliminary to the deeper understanding of this tremendous vista, it would be necessary to learn how Kundalini is aroused and directed to the various centres of the vehicles of a human being, not merely for a general vivification of their life, but also, as may be required, for their individual vivification to certain definite ends. For example, a lecture has to be delivered, an audience or congregation has to be influenced. Watching the process at work, it seemed as if it automatically begins by the general stimulation of Kundalini along, and up and down, the spine, so that there comes about a distinct glow. This happens to a microscopic extent with all who lecture, or who, in one or another of a number of ways, seek to influence for good their fellow-men. But where there is training the glow expands into a fire. And further results can be obtained if special vivification takes place in the heart, throat and along the line between the middle of the head and the centre of the eyebrows. This vivification proceeds through the solar plexus, a fact which partly accounts for the feeling of sickness some people experience before lecturing or before some other unusual strain, together with other physical symptoms. In special cases, such feelings always occur, marking the purification of the vehicles in order to facilitate the down-pouring of higher, and also of superhuman, Kundalini.

This does not mean that in most of these people Kundalini is actually aroused, but that there is in them a concentration, an intensification, of the universal Kundalini Fire, with the result that their nerves and other channels have more to carry than the Fire-load to which they are normally accustomed. However localized Kundalini may be from one point of view, from another it is universal - omnipresent. In some cases, however, the concentration of the Fire is predominantly local. It is a case of spontaneous combustion, but the same effects are noticeable.

It is clear that nicotine and alcohol definitely act in some way upon Kundalini, the former interposing a barrier between the general force of Kundalini and its operation in the various vehicles of the individual concerned, while the other seems to act as a direct stimulant, stirring the Force in wrong directions, or in some way wrongly intensifying it, and in any case doing these things in connection with an individual far from ready for Fire-development. All narcotics, drugs, stimulants, clog the system and interpose a deadening miasma between the individual and all larger consciousness.

But to return to the stimulation of Kundalini for special purposes, the spinal glow seems to be the first phenomenon, and this is intensified by external conditions - as, for example, presence in an already magnetized area, a church, a temple - or by the influence of music, chanting, participation in ceremony or service, and so forth. In addition to the stimulation of the spinal glow there is also an awakening, a glowing, as it were, of the heart, throat and middle-head centres, sometimes all together, sometimes one and not the rest, according to temperament. This stimulation often has a definite physical counterpart in the disturbance of organic functioning. The vivification of the heart centre seems to be - how otherwise to express it? - that of a cold glow. The juxtaposition of the two words sounds absurd. And yet I do not think the facts have been misinterpreted.

As regards the throat, the vivification, noticed on a particular occasion, seemed to express itself physically as a kind of momentary constriction, which was attributed to repercussions from the breaking down of barriers between the non-physical and the physical, so as to enable Kundalini to vivify the actual vibrations issuing from the throat as, for example, when a lecture is delivered. The result is an address potent apart altogether from any eloquence, and affecting in different ways people in the audience who are at different levels of evolution. They become bathed in Kundalini, the result in individual cases depending upon individual receptivity.

It becomes apparent that Kundalini may well be compared with electricity as to the uses to which it can be put. Continuous consciousness, remembrance of events during the night, and so on, are only certain fruits of the arousing of Kundalini. Even more important is the directly added power it gives for work in the outer world. It is both another sense and a very powerful stimulation of existing senses, as well as of all other forces the individual already wields. We are only at the beginning of discoveries regarding Kundalini, for the interesting effects observed are but the results of the earliest stages of its awakening, of the breaking down of preliminary barriers. Mercifully, the world is preserved from the discovery by science of the Kundalini Ray, or annihilation would ensue. When we read of the so-called " Death Rays " and other highly destructive emanations from great centres of Force, we may think of Kundalini as more powerful than all of them put together, and we shall be glad to leave it alone until it is necessary that we should learn to use it. It turns in boomerang fashion with terrible effect upon those who misuse it, upon those who do not reverence it, upon those who use it to selfish ends.

THE DANGERS OF KUNDALINI

CHAPTER 3

Much stress is, therefore, laid on the dangers of arousing Kundalini. Let us examine their nature. First and foremost there is the danger of sexual stimulation so that the individual becomes drained of his vitality through sex-obsession. Mental unhingement lies along this line. Sexual vitality and activity are very closely allied to Kundalini, for both are supremely creative in their nature, and the development of the one is bound to stir the development of the other. All sexual urge must be under complete control, at the will of the individual, and must be in a condition of what may be called sublimation, that is to say it must be recognized as a sacrament and therefore to be used in reverence and in a spirit of dedication. Sex-differentiation in all its various implications is one of God's earliest gifts to His children - often abused and grossly used, but at last learned to be approached as the true priest approaches the altar. Only those who thus approach the divinity of sex may be safely entrusted with that later gift of Kundalini, which can be handled with safety and profit by the tried and trusty alone.

Second, there is the danger of upsetting the physical rhythmic equilibrium through the uncontrolled stimulation of the various centres of the body - the possibility of injury to the heart, to the nervous system through the solar plexus, the individual becoming a chronic invalid with general physical deterioration of the brain, producing a strain also ending in mental unhingement. These dangers are avoidable provided the individual is in very sound health, has already gained an ample measure of self-control, thinks quietly and clearly, never narrowly, and is free from any servility to sexual impulses, has in fact little if any sexual tendency at all. It must be remembered that, however much he may be helped to awaken Kundalini, its development depends largely upon himself. He must watch the various symptoms and regulate them. How? He will know how, if he is ready for the awakening. No further guidance need be given here, for the sign of an individual being ready for the awakening of Kundalini lies in the intuitive knowledge of what to do, and in the help of the Wise.

We must never forget that the physical body is denser, and therefore less adaptable, than all others, and that there tends to arise a concentration of force in a particular area, not a general distribution over the whole. If we look at, say, the astral and mental bodies, we notice that each body is in one sense one great organ. Functions which to a certain extent are in the physical body associated with particular parts of the body are, in the case of the inner bodies, more universal. To a certain extent, perhaps, we may speak of localization in regard to the inner bodies, but it is more or less the whole of the astral body that feels, that receives impressions, that communicates. It is the same with the mental body. The whole of it thinks.

Now with the physical body, while feeling is distributed throughout, and while special centres are affected by feelings and sensations of an unusual kind, the brain acts as the principal channel of communication between the physical and astral bodies. Numb the brain, numb the nerves which communicate with the brain, and feeling disappears, so far as the waking consciousness is concerned, though its effects may remain, as witness the shock after an operation which, by reason of an anaesthetic, has been temporarily painless.

Similarly, it is the brain which is the main channel between the physical body and the mental body. I feel sure that the mental body impresses itself in some measure upon all parts of the physical body, so that all parts " think " to a certain extent, just as all parts feel. But the brain is the main centre, the great junction for the outer world. We may, therefore, visualize the inner bodies as exercising pressure throughout the physical body, but with the pressure greatest at the brain junction. The brain bears the brunt comparatively easily in normal cases and with the ordinary individual, since only very small channels are in fact allowed to be open between the various bodies.

But Kundalini will inevitably flow, apart from its normal channels, so as to vivify those centres which are most sensitive, have greatest receptivity. Hence the already existing concentration will be considerably intensified, generally when the organ involved is already bearing a full load. An individual in whom, for whatever cause, Kundalini tends to stir, is certainly living at what is to all intents and purposes high pressure. He is likely to be intensely alive. He is likely to have deep concentrations of force in his various organs, the concentrations varying in strength according to the use he makes of one rather than of another. Kundalini may very well be "the last straw," and hurl the unfortunate individual down into cruel darkness, if he be not a spiritual athlete trained to bear the strain.

Doubtless there will have come into existence, at this stage of the evolutionary process, channels between the inner worlds and the individual mainly Jiving in the outer world. But such channels are not likely to be deep, and if suddenly a rush of force whirls through one or another of them, or directly into a physical organ, they may well " burst," and bring about catastrophe.

When the physical, emotional and mental bodies are beginning to become resolved into their higher counterparts, as in the case of those who are concluding human existence so far as imprisonment in it is concerned, then Kundalini flows naturally and without encountering more than a minimum of obstruction. There is beginning to be but one Fire, one Life. It is at stages earlier than this that extreme circumspection is vital, for the Serpent-Fire does not discriminate. It consumes. It tends to flow along the lines of least resistance, and sometimes such lines may lead downwards and not upwards, with indescribably disastrous effect.

As development takes place, and as the higher consciousness gradually gains permanent ascendancy, the interpenetration becomes more rhythmic, and the whole of the lower agency responds far more immediately and richly to higher stimulation.

What then does the awakening of Kundalini effect? To all intents and purposes it breaks down barriers; or, to put this in another way, it flings wide open the sluice gates, which hitherto have been opening slowly and gradually, and which, in the case of the ordinary individual, are open only to a very limited extent. There begins to be complete communication between all the bodies, though the use and interpretation of such communication are necessarily a matter of some considerable time after the preliminary communication has been established. The lower bodies begin to reflect in increasing clarity the characteristics of the higher bodies - higher mental and lower Buddhic. States of consciousness begin to interpenetrate, so that there arises a hitherto unexperienced continuity of consciousness. This means enormously increased sensitiveness throughout all the bodies, demanding that large measure of self-control, which is so constantly emphasized.

Nowadays, in the case of many, Kundalini must be developed in the market-places, where the danger is great, and not in the forests, where the danger is minimized. Time is too precious for isolation from the world, especially in these days; and risks must be run. The whole of the physical body, becoming a wonderfully sensitive instrument, becoming refined out of all relation to its surroundings, can easily, therefore, be shaken to pieces as a result of the impact of coarse and violent vibrations from without. Sturdy physical health is thus a sine qua non for the arousing of Kundalini, and the health of an adult rather than that of a youth.

But there is still more. Though the whole of the physical body becomes enormously more sensitive, the brain has to bear the brunt. Pressure upon the physical brain is very greatly increased, since the brain is the main junction between the physical and the inner bodies. Can the brain stand the pressure? This is, perhaps, the principal question with regard to the arousing of Kundalini. The answer largely depends upon the extent to which the physical grey matter is sufficiently developed, steeled and reinforced, through self-control, to stand the strain. The condition and number of the spirillae are, perhaps, a determining factor, for these indicate the condition of the channels of contact and of what seems to be - I can think of no other words - the stretching power of the physical matter itself. It must be able to bend so that it may not break. I do not use the word " bend " literally, perhaps the word " adapt " would be more accurate. I think of the pressure from the inner bodies as in the nature of the flow of a fluid, of an almost irresistible flow. Can the brain shape itself to the flow, yield to it, adapt itself to it? If so, all may be well. But rigidity is fatal, and by rigidity I mean not merely, as it were, physical rigidity, but mental and emotional rigidity; that is to say, a crystallization or hardening of certain parts of the mental and emotional bodies, which hardening translates itself into the setting up within the brain, and indeed also within the heart, of grooves which will break but will not expand.

It is all a very complicated matter, for fundamentally the wisdom of arousing Kundalini depends largely, though by no means entirely, upon the condition of the lower mental and emotional bodies, and upon the extent to which the Causal and Buddhic vehicles are beginning to make contact and assert themselves. But physical conditions have also to be taken into account, though these are but reflections of inner conditions. The question then is: Are the inner bodies adequately developed and controlled, and is the physical vehicle recovered from such educative misuse as must inevitably have taken place during the long ages of development? For even though the physical body changes from life to life, as generally do the emotional and lower mental bodies, each new body is moulded to reflect, and to express, the stage of development reached. It may in fact be a case of the spirit being willing but the flesh being weak, a case of the Ego being ready but the lower bodies being weak, for the reason that the physical body in its existing condition is unable to stand the strain of Kundalini. In such cases, it may be necessary to wait for another life, so that existing forms may be broken up and more malleable forms substituted. It is clear from all this how complicated the process of the awakening of Kundalini really is, and how foolhardy an individual would be who sought to arouse it without wise sanction, and without a certain amount of guidance. It is almost certain he would come to terrible grief. Hence, the brain is a great danger-point, for disaster will be the result of an overstrained brain. The path of occultism, it is said, is strewn with wrecks. I venture to think that the path of the arousing of Kundalini, even if only in the very first stages, is strewn with even more wrecks.

> *A little learning is a dangerous thing;*
> *Drink deep, or taste not the Pierian Spring,*

said Pope. Before anyone seeks to arouse Kundalini let him know much about it, especially of its dangers, let him be intimately acquainted with these. He will then leave it alone until advised to begin. A little knowledge may incline him to foolishness. When he drinks deep he will realize that duty forbids experiment, the results of which, when made in ignorance, lead to disaster, first to the experimenter, which might not much matter one way or the other except to himself, but also to those immediately around him, and involving danger to the community as a whole - and to this he has no right to subject them.

KUNDALINI ACTIVE EVERYWHERE

CHAPTER 4

Take it that Kundalini is more or less active in all life. It is the Fire of Life, and therefore flows through all. But it may flow either as a gentle stream, simply vitalizing, or it may be directed into special channels and become a raging torrent, let us hope subordinated to great purpose, so that the raging is a purposeful, disciplined raging, though a raging none the less. Kundalini flows in mineral, vegetable, animal and human kingdoms, in ascending degrees of vitality, but, except in rare cases, as a gentle, fructifying stream of Fire, bathing as it were the whole of the vehicle

Each time, however, a distinct and definite advance takes place in spiritual growth, an intensification of Kundalini occurs, becoming particularly marked, though still generalized, in connection with the various stages leading to the Path and on the Path itself [1]. Relationship to a Master makes a marked difference in the virility of the flow, while entry into His consciousness, which takes place at the Accepted stage of discipleship, means the beginning of the definite, but still informal, harnessing of Kundalini to specific purposes, through the general influence of the Kundalini of the Master working on that of the apprentice. One of the reasons why the Master needs to be careful about admitting an apprentice to this close relationship of Accepted discipleship is this increased stimulation of Kundalini, even though it still remains general. The relation of Sonship is yet a further stimulation, while entry into the Great Brotherhood [2] is the beginning of the link between the Kundalini of the individual and that of the Brotherhood as a whole.

It must be remembered that the Great White Lodge is itself an individual, a specialized individual consciousness, with functions differentiated according to the various lines of its constituent parts. These differentiated functions may be regarded as the spiritual counterparts on an exalted scale of the various centres of the physical body. The mighty force of the Kundalini of the Brotherhood flows through these centres and through each member, so that admission to the Brotherhood involves participation in this great flow; the gradual uniting of the consciousness of the individual with the consciousness of the Brotherhood as a whole, involving a progressive uniting of the two Kundalinis. The Kundalini of the individual begins to enter the stream of the Brotherhood Kundalini. The converse process has, however, also to take place - the gradual entry of the Brotherhood Kundalini into the system of the individual, not merely in a general way, but highly specialized. I wonder whether, for the sake of accuracy, I ought not to speak of these more definite stages in the growth of Kundalini as the conscious directing of the Force, rather than as an " awakening ". Wherever there is life, there is Kundalini more or less awake, and awakening. But the conscious direction and handling of its power is another matter altogether.

One of the specially interesting effects of Kundalini is the intensification of the sense of unity to which its active stimulation gives rise. A breaker down of barriers between the various layers and states of consciousness, it is also the breaker of barriers between the individual himself and the larger Self without. The definite stimulation of Kundalini intensifies, for example, the individual consciousness of unity with the great consciousness of the Brotherhood as a whole. Through the operation of the Kundalini power the separated self begins to lose its illusion of separateness. The consciousness of the individual member of the Brotherhood is, of course, blended with that of the Brotherhood by very reason of his membership, but in many ways the blending is implicit rather than explicit, though explicitness grows with use of the Brotherhood power. But explicitness is very greatly hastened by the development of Kundalini, which works like The Theosophical Society in its First Object, for it bridges all distinctions of plane and consciousness.

Entry into The Theosophical Society very definitely effects a general, though probably in the vast majority of members no specific, stimulation of Kundalini. The Kundalini in the individual is definitely stirred, and its intensity augmented, for The Society, strange as it may seem, is a definite organism, and has its own mode of Kundalini. In some cases the stimulation proves too much to bear. The Theosophical Society inevitably attracts a few people who are somewhat unbalanced, just as it attracts the pioneer and those who have freed themselves from the ordinary conventional fetters. The Theosophical Society must ever be, to a certain extent, for people who are different, whether in one way or in another. Those who are different, because lacking in ordinary self-control, will probably find the stimulation more than they can bear. They are on the whole unlikely to grow better, and may quite likely grow worse. Those who are different because they have transcended ordinary limitations will benefit enormously. There are, however, more in whom there is a latent weakness, which the stirred Kundalini will intensify just as much as it will intensify a quality. Kundalini is power - power which can be used for good or ill. The weakness grows, the individual, of course, all the time regarding himself as the sole repository of truth and common sense. The strain grows to breaking-point, and the blessing conferred by membership of The Society, turned by uncontrolled weakness into a curse, is mercifully withdrawn through the removal of the individual from membership, doubtless in a cloud of self-righteousness from his standpoint, though in sadness from the standpoint of the Elder Brethren. The Society is naturally condemned in the particular way most conducive to the individual's self-satisfaction. In nine cases out of ten, it is pride which precedes the fall, and pride never knows itself as pride, or it would very properly commit suicide, as indeed it does in the case of common-sense people. Yet the Society goes on, grows in favour with the Hierarchy, increases in strength and usefulness.

That which I have written regarding The Theosophical Society is no less true in the case of other movements directly focusing upon the world the forces of Light in opposition to those of darkness. The facts are observed in connection with The Theosophical Society, but they are equally observable in very many other organizations, though to a lesser extent in most case.

Notes

1. By " the Path " I refer to that short cut up the mountain side of evolution whereby an individual, who has the necessary detachment from present circumstances and an adequate grasp of essential truth, may compress into a comparatively few lives the growth which ordinarily takes a century and more of incarnations. Mr. Lloyd George, the British statesman, said during the War that the world was traversing in a few years the distance which ordinarily it would take centuries to achieve. It is also possible to traverse in a few lives the spiritual distance which it would ordinarily take possibly thousands of years to achieve. But the help of a Master is needed, of One who Himself has achieved, has taken the short cut up the mountain side. Such an Elder Brother may from time to time apprentice to Himself persons "who show signs of being capable of enduring the hardships attendant on the heavy climbing - hardships which more often than not cause the would-be climber to decide to revert to the longer and easier route.

2. The Great Brotherhood, or Great White Lodge, consists in part of those highly evolved Souls who have reached that stage of the evolutionary pathway which gives them membership of what is called in occult literature the Inner Government of the world, and in part of those who, though far off from such a stage, are nevertheless sufficiently advanced to be trained to become members of this Government, compared with which all outer governments are but toy governments, in the future. Membership of the Great Brotherhood, or Great White Lodge, is open to the very earnest and faithful worker who has begun to know the nature and purpose of life. But he stands on the lowest rungs of the great Ladder of the Inner Life, is but a student of government, not a veritable Master in the science.

THE DEVELOPMENT OF KUNDALINI

CHAPTER 5

It is interesting to note the progress of a particular experience in developing Kundalini, or rather in stirring Kundalini into activity. In the particular case observed, the principal work is done during sleep, and appears at first to consist in the preparation of the spinal passage by moving Kundalini from the base of the spine to the top of the head. The individual out of the body can do this work, for though there are physical effects the Fire itself is non-physical. The globe or sphere at the base of the spine contains within it the Kundalini Fire coiled spherically. The prescribed concentration upon the globe, and thus upon the Fire within, begins to stir it into activity, provided the right kind of life has been lived beforehand for a considerable period, which is to say provided it is fed with the right kind of fuel. Even if the right kind of life has not been lived, a stirring may take place, but the effect of the premature stirring, if any take place at all, will be disastrous, as has already been pointed out.

Assuming the stirring takes place along right lines, there is a gradual dissolution of the globe caused by the frictional energizing of the Fire itself. The Fire is fanned into bright heat and becomes active, forcing its way through the matter in which it lies embedded, burning it up, and causing the globe to become a Radiant Sun, instead of the dull though glowing mass it normally is. This Sun radiates in all directions heat which is physically felt, specially in the surrounding areas of the physical body.

This Kundalini Sun would seem to rush upwards when it moves fast, as often it does not, along the spine as a bullet passes through a grooved gun-barrel. There is something spiral about the movement. In any case, there seems to be a direct rush upwards, without passing beyond the top of the head, but specially stimulating centres according to the individual's Ray. The sensation is that of pressure, while as regards the centre at the top of the head unusual heat will be felt.

During the waking hours this process may be continued, and from time to time it seems to occur of itself, so that a warm glow passes up the spine, producing a most interesting effect. A beautiful expansion of consciousness is physically experienced, so that the individual feels full of a glorious life and of a sense of intimate contact with what must be the developed intuitive consciousness. He imagines what life would be like if he could keep this experience constant, instead of only intermittent. There is a fine sense of at-one-ment, of radiance, of contact with the Real. Barriers seem to have been broken down, so that the individual sees into the heart of things, no matter what they are, and sees them as growing entities, their glorious future disclosed to him as embryonic in them. It is so difficult to describe this condition of consciousness, but the physical, indeed much more than the physical, seems transcended, and some veils at least are lifted so that he gazes upon a Real, less hidden by the clouds of illusion.

In the beginnings of this process a certain amount of dizziness is noticeable. A new constituent has become active. It is as if a new dimension had opened out, so that a new world is entered. The dizziness is perhaps the physical expression of a new relativity, of a new adjustment, other worlds than the physical beginning to be open to a gaze which the individual has not yet learned to control, so that he looks out as it were with all " eyes " vaguely open, instead of with those appropriate to the particular plane on which he happens to be dominantly functioning. Later on he will be able to close the eyes he does not need, leaving open only those he does. And later on still, he will be able, perhaps, to use all " eyes " simultaneously, each " eye " dovetailing into the others, so as to avoid distortion and flickering between one state of consciousness and another - the effect being the dizziness.

Yet another effect, presumably only in the earlier stages, is that of seeming to be elsewhere. The individual feels as if he were living elsewhere, so that the outer world seems to be at a distance. He is far away, and the noise and rush of life come to him only as a faint murmur. He is as a spectator at a play, and he looks at the players on the stage as denizens of a world other than his world. This sensation is more or less continuous, and invests the outer world with a peculiar unreality, the physical expression of which is the hearing of the world as if muted. It is almost as it he were deaf. He looks out upon the world as if he had no concern with it. His physical brain is in one sense numbed, definitely numbed, though at the same time it is extraordinarily alert to the Real, full of a hitherto unexperienced keenness, fire, clarity. It is beautifully stimulated. There seem to be momentary flickers from far-away consciousness, so that a flash of other-consciousness occurs from time to time, though only shadowy. This flash seems to take place when there is special warmth at the top of the head, possibly the result of a little escape of Kundalini Fire.

Sensitiveness is enormously increased, chiefly in the region of the spine, though to a certain extent throughout the whole body. A loud noise seems to grate as upon a raw spine, and sends a shock through the whole body. A special jar may cause a kind of inner dislocation for quite a while. This sensitiveness has the further effect of making the individual a kind of sensitive plate upon which, for example, people in the outer world imprint themselves, so that in a flash he knows their natures, specially the high lights of quality and the low lights of defect. He will at once have either a positive or a negative impression. The former will be positively good or positively unfavourable, and in either case general tendencies will be perceived, though not perhaps the details. Sometimes there is nothing about the person worth considering, there is nothing to be noted about him one way or the other. He is ordinary, and may for some time longer be left to the nursing of the ordinary circumstances of life. But one knows as in a flash, even though details may not be forthcoming.

As time passes the whole body seems to glow with Fire, which one imagines to extend some distance, so that a person very near should almost feel the glow and become stimulated by it. The process is temporarily fatiguing to the physical body, and it is pleasant to lie down. Does the Fire glow more easily when the spine is in a recumbent position? I am inclined to think that the restriction of the Fire, so that ordinarily it does not pass beyond the top of the head, tends to exercise pressure upon the physical brain and induce somnolence.

SUN-KUNDALINI
AND
EARTH-KUNDALINI

CHAPTER 6

How wonderful a difference the stirring of Kundalini makes as regards sensitiveness to influence either emanating from a centre or aroused by activity, as for example in a Church service ! To go into a city is to feel as if every vital part drooped, as flowers droop for want of air. Under stimulating influences, such as proximity to a centre of spiritual vitality, to some temples and churches, or the taking part in ceremonial activities, or in meetings highly charged with uplifting influences, the centres seem to unfold as a flower opens to the Sun, and Kundalini glows throughout the body. And this unfoldment and glow make contact between the lower and higher bodies, bringing into the lower the influences of the higher. In the beginning of Kundalini development it is at once a pain and a glory to contact such spiritual influences - a pain because Kundalini has not yet overcome the obstacles to its unfoldment, a glory because the Fire of Life Eternal is flowing through every vehicle, and for the time being one lives in the larger consciousness. On occasions there will be an immediate intensification of Kundalini from the base of the spine, and a beautiful glow which serves to intensify identification both with the aspiration, which the occasion may have released, and with the descent of blessing for which the aspiration has become the channel.

There seem as if there are two sources of Kundalini, or perhaps it would be more accurate to say that

Kundalini plays between two poles, one positive - the Sun, one negative - the Earth, at all events so far as regards our particular evolution. The Rod of Power, well known to the deeper students of occultism, seems both to symbolize this fact and to express it. The negative Earth globe at one end, the positive Sun globe at the other, and the Fire in each and in-between. To hold the Rod of Power is to grasp the Power of God. Few there be who may touch it. It is a focus on occasions of stupendous outpourings of Force.

The heart of the Earth is one pole of Kundalini, the heart of the Sun is the other. Now the awakening of Kundalini is tantamount to a fashioning of a shadow of the Rod between the globes. In one sense one ever is a Rod, but the Rod is not yet awake. It is asleep or dreaming, and the Fire itself slumbers. To awaken Kundalini is to fan the Fire into a consuming Flame, burning, purifying, energizing, making conscious contact with the Universal Fire.

To awaken Kundalini is to draw the Fire " from Earth beneath," " from Heaven above," so that the bodies, including the physical, become as a Rod between the two great centres. The individual, as it were, steps consciously into the space between the centres and becomes charged with the interplay of force, with Kundalini.

Let me try to visualize the process. I have written above of concentration on the base of the spine. But the base of the spine is in fact but a receiving station, a centre of distribution. From the centre of the Earth and from the Sun we draw the Kundalini power. We concentrate it at the spine-base centre and send it on its vitalizing way through the great centres of being. Up flows Kundalini from the Earth, through feet and limbs, through the negative creative energy, the centre of physical creation, into the globe at the base of the spine which represents and unifies both Sun and Earth. Down flows Kundalini from the Sun, its overwhelming intensity tempered as it adapts itself to the undeveloped mortal man. Upward flows a stream of Fire. Downward flows a stream of Fire. And the streams meet at the spine base to weld as it were into a spear of concentrated Force to travel upward on its appointed way! Think of the beautiful concentration of the mighty Jumna and the majestic Ganga at Allahabad, whence they flow united down to the sea from which in very truth they came. So do Earth-Kundalini and Sun-Kundalini meet in the globe at the root of the spine, thence flowing as one great Force into the Real, upon their surface the individual himself being carried onward into the Light. The negative Earth and the positive Sun combine, and spiritual Power is the fruition of the two.

In some ways, of course, this description is very inaccurate. Perhaps the truth would lie in the suggestion that both negative and positive slumber, as it is well they should, until both are stirred into life. The negative is no less valuable than the positive. Each has its part to play, its work to do.

Thus the individual, not merely his physical body but all his bodies - more the non-physical bodies than the physical body - becomes a Rod between the globes, between Earth and Sun.

At this point the student finds entering into the perspective of his vision the great triple Fire symbolized in the Caduceus. The Caduceus Fire and that of Kundalini lie close and together, forming a splendid rainbow of colour. They subserve the same ends - differently.

There is intimate connection between the Caduceus formed of the central line of force and its male and female intertwining aspects and the Fire of Kundalini. Though from one point of view the two forces are distinct, from another they are complementary and one might even almost say identical, being reflections of the Activity facet of the Diamond of Fire.

The Caduceus seems independently awakenable, that is to say, stirred into conscious usage on the part of the individual. But its relationship with Kundalini is intimate.

The student whose experiences are here recorded was unable to pursue further the intricacies of the relationship and respective functionings of the Caduceus Fire and the Kundalini Fire. But in Theosophical literature these are examined. All he could see was a stream of Fire, differently-hued, flowing from the root of the spine up into the head, with subtle connections maintaining ever open channels between those macrocosmic forces of which it is a current. It was very easy to confuse the Caduceus force with the force of Kundalini, for there is an eternal alliance between them; and the beginner always tends to perceive sameness before he notices differences. The student concerned had the distinct impression that while the Fire of the Caduceus offered a Way of Release, the Fire of Kundalini offered a Way of Fulfilment. Phrases in these regions must never be taken very literally, for here there are no impenetrable compartments, each aloof from all the rest. But it seemed as if Sushumna with its Ida and Pingala aspects, the Caduceus, were a route of release from confinement within the lower bodies, while the Fire of Kundalini is rather in the nature of a witness-guide to the identity of the larger with the smaller consciousness. The difference may be subtle, and from a functional point of view somewhat unreal. Yet it seems definite and probably has foundation in a fact not as yet clearly perceptible. Of some very close relationship between the two Fires there seems no doubt.

Meditation on these two Fires was provocative of imaginings, speculations, which tended to get out of hand - naturally so, since contact had been established with Cosmic Power, and there was a temporary illumination of the individuality with Cosmic Light. Immediately there was a sense of a swinging between the positive and negative forces of Fire Light-Life - Earth and Sun. Are there negative and positive centres in all individualities, human, nonhuman, super-human, sub-human? May we divide the centres we know according to their Earth-nature or their Sun-nature? Is the throat an Earth-centre, and the heart a Sun-centre? But such speculations lead the student into channels of investigation which for the time being are distinctly unprofitable.

THE HIGH PURPOSE
OF KUNDALINI

CHAPTER 7

The process of working up and down the spine having been begun, the next business is to set up movement between the various centres. The first valid centre is the solar plexus, and communication is to be established between the base of the spine and the solar plexus, round about the navel. The touching of the solar plexus gives rise to the same sensation of expansion of consciousness as in the case of the spinal movement. The stomach may, and probably will, feel some disturbance, a sickish feeling. But that does not matter. The student did not trace how the Force reaches the solar plexus, but it seems to be by a roundabout way.

Whenever a centre is vitalized with the Fire there is a sense of expansion of consciousness and of highly stimulated faculty, and particularly is the intuition developed since there is greatly increased contact between the higher and the lower bodies, the higher fortunately being able to dominate, or the process of arousing Kundalini would not have been permitted.

As it is, not only is there absence of the slightest sexual disturbance, but such remnants of sex-nature as there may have been seem to be transmuted and transformed into their true purpose - virility and creativeness, and thus Godliness. Instead of being confined within localized creative power which partly assumes the form of sex-impulse, life begins to dwell in the universal creative principle, in the Fire of Creation : the lower ascends into the higher, the particular into the universal. And when the particular becomes lost in the universal, thereby discovering its true Eternity, then the universal descends to take up its abode in the individual. This is part of the objective of Kundalini.

It is sometimes thought that the development of Kundalini leads to clairvoyance and continuous interplane consciousness, or to the linking of the various levels of consciousness, so that other states of consciousness may be connected with the waking consciousness. This does take place in due course, but of far greater importance is a very real transsubstantiation, the higher consciousness becoming jewels in the setting of the lower, the higher taking up its abode in the lower, that is to say in the waking consciousness itself. The lower knows itself to be a setting, and offers its substance for the jewels of the higher. This is in fact a setting up of continuous consciousness. Whether in fact clairvoyance, etc., arises or not, though in course of time it will, is of far less importance than the definite establishment of the higher consciousness - Buddhic and later Nirvanic - in the waking consciousness, this being the high purpose of the arousing of Kundalini. This means, as has been said, an extraordinary vivification of intuition - pure knowledge untainted, undistorted, by the personal equation; for into awakened Buddhic and Nirvanic consciousness no un-universalized personal equation can ever enter. The personal equation is transcended, the desires of the lower self begin to be transmuted into the Will of the One Great Self. We may trust to an intuition vivified, purified, by Kundalini, but we must take care that we allow no outside considerations to distort. If we dwell in the realm of pure intuition our conclusions are likely to be true. Let us trust first impressions provided we sense them as coming from the depths of our being and not from the shallows. The arousing of Kundalini should establish us permanently in the Real - this is its supreme objective, all other results can only be incidental to this great end.

There seem to be two general systems of Kundalini development; one which proceeds slowly, very slowly, and carefully, little by little, perhaps extending over lives, the various psychic faculties being developed *pari passu* with general growth; the other being to leave the positive arousing of Kundalini until the last moment, so to speak, and then, when all is safe and the word of the Master has gone forth, to arouse Kundalini with a rush. This method has in one sense more of risk in it, but there should not be any if the individual is alert. I am reminded of the launching of a ship. She goes down, gradually increasing in speed, into the sea, but only after all details of the slipway are attended to with most meticulous care. But once she is set going she quickly takes the plunge. In some cases, this latter method is employed, in others, the former.

As a setting for the right development of Kundalini, there is always an extraordinary desire to use the intensified power to help others. There is often the deliberate turning of oneself into a negative photographic plate, " exposing " it to those nearby, that their needs may be directly known. This longing to be of service to others is greatly stimulated, and indeed much more help can be given, because of the vivified intuition. One even feels inclined to advise some of one's friends, if they ask, quite frankly as to what they need, the advice being available because the individual has discerned so very clearly, with the aid of Kundalini, what he himself needs. He can help others because he has discovered how to help himself. But discretion and tact are the better part of valour, and one must not hinder in the effort to be helpful.

CENTRES AND FUNCTIONS
OF KUNDALINI

CHAPTER 8

More advanced students often show the student a number of ways of using Kundalini, which, by the way, seems crimson in colour. One method is of drawing a pupil into the teacher's own Kundalini-infused aura, so that he takes, as it were, a Kundalini bath. This is a potent vitalization, and does no harm at all, provided the teacher takes care, as he does, to see that in the individual there are no prominent characteristics which might be undesirably intensified by Kundalini stimulation. It should be remembered that to bathe in Kundalini does not involve the arousing of Kundalini, for in one way we are all bathing in Kundalini, the vital principle, Bergson's elan vital. But to admit a person to a bath of what may be called concentrated Kundalini demands care. It might be suitable for an undeveloped person of an unobjectionable disposition, and also for a developed person who has already learned to dominate his lower nature.

One of the reasons at any rate why the Elder Brethren are unable to live in the outer world is the effect upon the average individual of Their supremely dynamic Kundalini. We know how a wireless station, for example, seems charged with electricity - the air being full of it. Some people are adversely affected by this electrical atmosphere. Similarly, in far more intense degree, many people would be even dangerously affected by the physical propinquity of an Elder Brother dynamic with Kundalini Fire. The world is not yet ready for such stimulation. Consider the effect the Christ had upon the people 2,000 years ago even though He used the body of a disciple. The Kundalini Fire in the disciple, inevitably intensified by the immediate presence of the Christ, fired the people one way or the other, and finally the other. There was inadequate self-control to stand the strain of the searching penetration of Kundalini. We have been told that this was anticipated, and that the work planned was fulfilled when a few disciples became available to transmit the Christ's Message to future generations. No more was expected from the people of the time, or perhaps not much more, for it was realized that the force introduced into their midst would probably be too much for them. Yet, for the sake of the few who could be inspired to pass on the Message to unborn generations, the risk of non-acceptance and of the murder of the physical vehicle of the Lord had to be run. May it not be that the karma of the Jews is not so heavy as might otherwise be imagined, for they were face to face with a Force the effects of which even the Love of the Christ Himself could not neutralize, or should I rather say, turn aside, transmute or veil?

Kundalini Fire is the essence of the Love of God, so that there can be no question of neutralization, but only of, as it were, protecting the eyes from a blinding Light. This could not be perfectly done 2,000 years ago.

In this connection, there are a number of complicated considerations into which I need not enter. One, for example, is the extent to which constant and immediate contact with crowds has to be avoided, much of the work being done from centres, rather than in the midst of the people.

The Word of a Saviour thus descends into the future partly through His life in His disciples, partly through transmission by disciples and through books, but largely, mainly, through highly charged Kundalini centres, Kundalini thus concentrating in special areas on the surface of the earth : bathing pools of Fire, spiritual bathing pools, as they indeed become, as well as centres for the emanation of the Fire throughout the world.

To return to the methods of using Kundalini another way seemed to be that of directing a stream through the head of an individual, through what seemed to be a funnel-shaped opening, so that the stream floods the body, or rather the bodies. This is a safe method of using the Force since it reflects the principle of fructification, which is ever from above - sunshine, rain, etc. Care must, however, be taken that the Force thus employed is adapted in intensity to the receptivity of the individual. Some people may be able to stand a tropical storm, but the majority need but gentle rain.

A third method of the use of this Fire is in the case of protection against machinations of Brethren of the Shadow. A student came across a case of an undesirable person who was inciting people to commit suicide, and had even urged them to the point of hanging cords around their necks. The law allowed him in this case to spray upon the undesirable individual, or possibly " thought-form " emanating from an undesirable individual, a piercing stream of crimson Fire. In the case of the form, it was at once destroyed, thus instantly freeing the victims from their obsession. What was the nature of the repercussion upon the individual himself? Probably illness, possibly disintegration. A curious feature of the process seemed to be that the Fire was directed from a centre. It seems as if Kundalini can be sent forth from any centre, though preferably from the solar plexus centre or from the centre between the eyebrows. We thus begin to realize that the great centres of the body are the main distributors of force. It is not a matter of eyes or hands or feet, but of centres.

THE INDIVIDUALITY OF KUNDALINI

CHAPTER 9

Curiously enough, even though there seems to be obstruction at the top of the head, not in the centre of the head but actually at the top, nevertheless to a certain extent Kundalini pierces its way through and ascends through the top of the head beyond the physical body like a fountain of coloured water. The result is a stream which opens out so that there is the appearance of a tunnel, Kundalini flowing outwards, as it were, over the edge of the funnel. In the beginning this funnel emerges only a short distance, but as the piercing process proceeds the force of the stream becomes greater and Kundalini rises to a great height. All head obstructions vanish, with the result that contact is made, a channel pierced, between the various types of consciousness, leading to continuous consciousness and to constant contact between the various planes and the physical-brain waking consciousness.

What is the nature of the obstruction at the top of the head? It has the appearance of a mass of grains of " sand," yellowish in colour, through which Kundalini is endeavouring to effect a permanent passage, tearing apart the mass, making a hole through it, a process of some difficulty, some pain, and a certain amount of danger. At first, Kundalini only glows. As time passes, the glow must become a burning nucleus and later a consuming, purifying and releasing fire. These grains of " sand " presumably are cells, and they are not so close to one another that Kundalini cannot effect some sort of a passage, just as water can escape through a sieve.

It is interesting to watch the nature of the process of awakening Kundalini as it takes place during the sleep of the physical body. The most interesting observation is as to the density or solidity of Kundalini itself. From one standpoint, Kundalini is a Fire, liquid Fire, but from another there is an exact simile in the planting of a long pole in a hole in the ground. The earth has to be hollowed out and the pole inserted into the hole thus made.

Similarly, in the lower bodies obstruction has to be removed from the course Kundalini must take - obstruction both physical, etheric, and possibly higher as well; and the picture the student had in his mind's eye as he awoke is of digging away varying densities of solids so that another kind of solid may enter the passage thus cleared. One might well employ the simile of boring into the earth. In the course of the process earth is encountered, earth and water are encountered, then perhaps water alone, and if one went far enough down one would meet molten masses and gases of various kinds. Now boring upwards has to take place for Kundalini, and the same kinds of obstructions are encountered, different kinds of solids even though we call them solids, liquids, gases, and so on. All are solids. Kundalini is a solid, and if it is to do its work, certain other kinds of solids must be removed out of the way. Not that it cannot more or less interpenetrate them.

It can and does permeate them to a certain extent. But its main objective cannot be accomplished unless it has a clear passage, and this involves the removal, perhaps only to a very small extent, of physical obstruction, possibly a heaping to either side, just as a crowd has to give way before an oncoming procession. There is probably partly a burning away and partly this crowding on either side.

As the channel is formed the pole of Kundalini is pushed up - a matter of time. The idea of Kundalini as a pole being gradually inserted into a hole seems to be more accurate than at first sight may appear. The distinctions we make between solids, liquids and gases, and so on, are relative terms. There are solids to which the most solid things we know are supremely light and airy. Some of these solids one notices in the inner regions of the earth. This is one way of regarding solids. Another way is to look upon the increasingly Real as, in the truest sense of the word, "solid," increasingly solid, substantial. From this point of view, Kundalini is more solid than the most solid substance we know, using the word "solid" as synonymous for "real".

Dealing with Kundalini in these terms one is conscious of its solidity as compared with that of physical matter or of substances next in degree of solidity, from the physical plane standpoint, to physical matter. Kundalini seems much more solid than these, and the process of awakening Kundalini may thus be not at all inaptly compared with the removal of earth, and of earth mixed with water, for the entry of a pole of solid wood, as has already been suggested. The pole of solid wood is relatively far more solid than earth or water. So is Kundalini from a certain point of view far more solid than the obstructions which have to be removed. I am not surprised, therefore, that the translation into terms of waking consciousness of the digging process, taking place during the sleep of the physical body, is that of the removal of earth and water so that a hole may be made for the entry of a very solid object indeed. In one sense, mental matter is much more "solid" than emotional matter, Buddhic more "solid" than mental, Nirvanic than Buddhic; just as space may be considered more solid than that which fills it. What we call matter can only be where the more solid so-called " space " is not there to prevent its presence. We have to drive away space in order to make room for matter. But sometimes we must drive away matter in order to make room for space, and this is what we are doing when arousing Kundalini, for Kundalini belongs, relatively, more to space than to matter.

There are speculations about Kundalini in which one is almost afraid to indulge. Universal, Cosmic Fire as it is, nevertheless it seems to be constituted of innumerable diverse elements, and one or another of these shines forth according to the setting of the Fire in individualities belonging to one or another of the great evolutionary streams. Each centre represents a line of energy, and in each individuality, therefore, one centre is dominant, while another comes next in importance. So is it that Kundalini adapts itself - I ought, of course, to say herself - to the pre-eminent note, and seems as if it energized the various centres according to their respective importances in the particular human body. It courses lightly, as it were, through the sub-dominant centres, touching them to minor vivification only, but giving radiance indeed to the centres which have special preeminence. And this principle obtains throughout the evolutionary process, in the vast macrocosms no less than in the minutest microcosms.

But Kundalini definitely stimulates each centre, whirling as each already is, throbbing and piercing its way upwards to the great head junction. There seems to be little doubt that there is a spiral, corkscrew movement of Kundalini as it surges upwards, concentrating on the centres which are outstanding because of the individual's Ray[1] and temperament, and sometimes vivifying certain centres which need special stimulation in view of certain work the individual has to undertake. Here one centre is stimulated more than the rest. There another centre is singled out. And perceiving this one wonders if nations and races, faiths and sects, have their super-ordinate centre as well as their subordinate centres, so that the Fire of Kundalini has to be all things to all centres.

One wonders if the same be true of land, of sea, of valley, of mountain, of forest, of plain. And then comes the speculation as to the supreme Centre of the Earth. The Earth, as we are told, has its colour, its note. Has it not its special centre also? This seems to be without doubt, as must also be the case with the Sun, with a Solar System, in fact with every organism. And when one tries to follow this speculation with the inner vision one becomes lost in regions of consciousness which forbid exploration, and one turns back wisely, though regretfully, into those realms which are, as these others are not yet, for our conquering.

The burning sensation, so usually associated with Kundalini, and by no means confined within the channels of its passage through the body, is not necessarily inevitable. There may be a sensation of cold, of pressure, of a bursting, the latter generally within the head. Some students have experienced an uncomfortable warmth throughout the trunk of the body, with extension into the head, so that the whole of the upper part of the body seems intensely hot, streaming forth heat in all directions.

But always, and this is an acid test of the rightness of the experience, the whole body becomes comparatively universalized as to its sensitiveness. The whole body becomes, as it were, a Gauge of the Real, so that discrimination, as has been said before, is alive from the feet to the very top of the head itself. This is a reflection on the physical plane of the absence in the inner bodies of the localization of faculties which is so apparent in the physical body itself. There arises, with the vivification of Kundalini, a blending of the lower with the higher bodies, so that there begins to be one vehicle - receptive and active in every part of its being.

In the higher regions of consciousness we cease to speak of vehicles, for the place of these is taken by radiances; and when Kundalini is still further developed, the consciousness which in the physical body has localizations, and in the higher bodies is co-extensive with their frontiers, will, in the highest regions, become concentrated in a centre, whence rays will issue forth in all directions.

Evolution consists in a going forth into the whole of manifested life, in contacting the farthest circumferences; but the way of return is to bring back, stage by stage, to the Centre the fruits of the going forth, the sum total of all the experiences. Thus do we seem to come to the point of concluding that in some mysterious way Kundalini remains for ever individual to its recipient, however much it may always be inseparable from the Universal Fire whence it issues forth. In some mysterious way it would seem as if Kundalini partakes of the nature of the Permanent Atom[2], cannot disintegrate, and forms the eternal Fire of the evolving individuality.

I have said that it cannot disintegrate. From one point of view nothing disintegrates. All that anything can do is to return home awhile, and this is what Kundalini probably does. The coursing of Kundalini through the centres of the body, its picking out a special centre or centres for major vivification, its issuing forth from the head, its unificatory powers - all are the gathering of experience for the Fire which is the individual himself.

We must, it seems clear, free ourselves from the habit of looking upon our bodies as just flesh and blood, as just matter, as matter is known in these days of feeble vision. All things are modes of manifestation of each other. All are modes of the manifestation of Fire, or of any other supreme expression of the Creative Spirit which we may be able to conceive. In Christian scriptures we have the conception of Fire as the third aspect of the Trinity, God the Holy Ghost. But behind all divisions there is the One without a Second, and true indeed is it that all that we can predicate of the expressions of the One we can predicate still more of the One Itself. So, from one aspect we may express the Creative Spirit as Fire, and all that comes from it as Fire no less. Hence we think of Kundalini as the heart, the permanent Fire, of the vehicles of an individual, and we think we see in the Permanent Atom the Fire of Kundalini awaiting its next forthgoing.

There seem to be inbreathings and outbreathings, pulsations of Kundalini. Observation seems to show that all things breathe, and that there are the most marvellous interpretations to be assigned to these breathings. The intensity of Kundalini waxes and wanes. It rises and falls, even in its surgings. It is exceedingly difficult to follow all this, for the student who has been observing is inexperienced, and in addition is confronted with the intensifications produced in his own Kundalini by the very observations themselves. Attention feeds, as inattention starves; and these constant experiences and experiments increase his own Kundalini activity. In these waxings and wanings Kundalini is evidently profoundly affected by the surroundings of the body in which it dwells. In the great open spaces, in the harmonious, rhythmic and well-ordered home, at sea, in close proximity to hills and mountains, in special gatherings of an uplifting nature, in well-directed ceremonial gatherings, in churches, temples and mosques round which fine devotion has gathered, in schools and colleges from which all fear is entirely absent and there subsists a beautiful relationship between teachers and taught : in all these, and other conditions of the same type, as in places of study, Kundalini waxes. But in towns and cities, in crowded places, in theatres, restaurants, picture-houses, in the ordinary public meeting devoid of any particular aspirational element, Kundalini wanes, that is to say it receives no stimulus. But always is there a tide in the affairs of Kundalini, an ebbing and a flowing, a rising and a falling, however imperceptible. It would seem doubtful if ever Kundalini is actually asleep, however inactive it may appear to be, for it must needs share the functioning of Kundalini everywhere, and as a whole Kundalini is astir throughout the spaces. Nevertheless, we feed Kundalini, and we starve Kundalini, in the veriest trifles of our living - physical, emotional, mental and beyond.

One observation which was of tremendous interest to the student making all these contacts was the use of what is called the Thyrsus in the special awakenings of Kundalini which from time to time take place. The Thyrsus has the magnetic property of reaching out into intimate touch with Kundalini and of causing Kundalini to follow it as iron is attracted by a magnet. In the ancient days the Thyrsus was very well known, and was evidently used in cases where a kind of artificial stimulation of Kundalini was indicated. It was certainly known to the Yogis of old in India, and to the Egyptians and the Greeks. The Thyrsus observed was manufactured of some brilliantly white metal, cylindrical in shape, about twenty-four inches long, an inch or so in diameter, and resembled nothing so much as the ordinary ruler. It was placed at the root of the spine and then drawn upwards, Kundalini following after it. Of course, the Thyrsus could only be used by those who already had an intimate knowledge of the workings of Kundalini.

Notes

1. Theosophy teaches that all life, whether in mineral, plant, animal or man, is the One Life. This One Life, long before it begins its work in mineral matter, differentiates itself into seven great streams, each of which has its own special and unchanging characteristics. These fundamental types are known as the Rays. These seven types are to be found among men, and we all belong to one or other of them. Fundamental differences of this sort in the human race have always been recognized; a century ago men were described as of the lymphatic or the sanguine type, the vital or the phlegmatic; and astrologers classify us under the names of the planets as Jupiter men, Mars men, Venus or Saturn men, and so on.

2. The central nucleus of each of man's bodies is a Permanent Atom, so-called because it remains ever within the periphery of the higher aura, even when the body itself has disintegrated. At rebirth, from this atom emanates a web-like substance into which the actual atomic particles of the new body are builded. The use of the permanent atoms is to preserve within themselves, as vibratory powers, the results of all the experiences through which they have passed. We must not think of the minute space of an atom as crowded with innumerable vibrating bodies, but of a limited number of bodies, each capable of setting up innumerable vibrations.

THE MUSIC OF KUNDALINI

CHAPTER 10

Can we describe the great Serpent-Fire of Kundalini in its fundamental glories, in its colours, in its shapes, in its music-notes? Can we describe its song? Can we describe its rainbow?

Kundalini is music as it is colour. It is a rainbow as it is a perfect song. The student senses this as he enters into its nature. Kundalini comes from afar, trailing clouds of colour and of sound. Kundalini is a perfect fruition of Life. It is a consummation of Life. It vibrates with consummated experience. Whose experience? The experience of One who has been one, but who has resolved into glory upon glory the unfoldments of His evolutionary way- unfoldments in darkness and in light, in peace and in storm, in joy and in sorrow. He has sown experiences, and He has reaped Flowers, a Garden of Flowers, Flowers that sing, Flowers that breathe forth colour.

Could the student but hear the Song of Kundalini, could he but " see " the colours of the Fire, he would know what Life is, for he would be penetrating into the very heart of Being. But his senses are dull, even those with the aid of which he experiments and experiences. He can know that which to him is knowable, and he can see as through a mist the as yet unknowable, and through the mist comes the glory of a throbbing majesty of sound - a single world-encircling, world-drenching throb of sound, yet containing within itself a veritable world of music. Through the mist, too, comes the glory of a mighty rainbow of colour, no less world-encircling and world-drenching. All is alive with colour-sound, colour singing, song colourful.

The student feels he may not suggest either a colour or a note as expressive of Kundalini, for each of us hears himself differently, sees himself differently, in this magic crystal of blended colour-sound. Let each listen. Let each see. It were almost a blasphemy to dim the crystal from its all-embracing purity.

Yet our Kundalini, the Cosmic Kundalini from our Lord the Sun and the individual Kundalini from our Mother the Earth, has its note dominant, different from the notes dominant of other modes of evolution, and is a blend of the Song of the Sun and the Song of the Earth. Our Lord the Sun sings His Song for all His universe. Our Mother the Earth sings her answering note, the note of life unfolding on her bosom. So does our Lord the Sun send forth His colour, and our Mother the Earth shines, in all her colour, radiance in answering homage.

How near sometimes the student seems to come to the song of Kundalini from the Sun, to the colour of it, and to the song of Kundalini from the Earth, to the colour of it. He sees at once that the Earth is but an image of the Sun her Father. The song of the Earth, the colour of the Earth, are but immature shadows of that coming substance perfectly resplendent in the Sun. He sees that all the singing from the Earth, and all the colour-messages, are but praise to the Lord of all, and from the heights of man in all his trappings of bodies right down to the humblest atom in the lowest of nature's kingdoms the student hears a song of praise and colour-throbbings of aspiration. Our Lord the Sun has set them all afire. He has set them all a-singing. He has set them all a-shining in a myriad hues. In their joy, in their deep consciousness that as He is so shall they be through the mystery of His Being in colour and in sound, they give to Him that which they have received from Him. Our Songs, our Colours, our Life, our Light, our Glory, are from Him, and we lift up our gifts that He may see we cherish them.

Kundalini sings to the student with the voice of all that lives. The student thus begins to know all life, not by a forthgoing, but by an indrawing. In the hidden recesses of his own Kundalini, if the possessive be pardoned, he finds the secret of the Unity of Life, as he has known Life's solidarities without.

There is a Unity, and it sings one song, composed though the song be of an infinitude of notes. There is a Unity, and it sends forth one colour, composed though it be of an infinitude of colours. There is but one song, but one colour, for all life on this Kundalini-Globe we call the Earth. In the Kundalini we hear the song, we see the colour. And when we are able to make external that which for so long must remain internal, and remote and inaccessible, only now and then revealing itself, when at last we are the Unity, then do we pass beyond the human kingdom, as we have passed beyond the kingdoms below, and the Kingship of the Matter-World is ours.

Kundalini is indeed vocal. She can be heard by those who have the ears to hear. She is substantial, even though yet more spatial, and can be seen by those who have the eyes to see. Kundalini is no mere fanciful abstraction. She is no mere theory, no mere externalization of an imaginative outpouring. She lives. She sings. She arrays herself in scintillating colours.

When we seek her within ourselves, and perchance catch a glimpse, be it in her sleep or in her stirrings, of her compassionate elusiveness, then if our eyes and ears be but faintly open, we shall see her raiment and hear her voice. And these shall be our raiment and our voice, not as these are now, but as these shall be some day. Is it not worth while to seek her, not by striving to awaken her before her rightful sleep is over, not by disturbing her if on occasion she sallies forth within the domain which is hers to illumine, but just by watching, as this student has watched, respectfully, without a ripple of desire for response?

The way to seek her is to detach oneself from one's anchorages, to break the bars of all imprisonments of physical body, feelings and emotions, and mind, and to lose oneself in the formless spaces of Life's infinitudes. It is needful to " feel" the infinitudes in their limitless natures, not going forth infinitely far, but being infinitely still. There is no far nor near when perfect stillness is achieved. Yet the stillness is vocal. It is supremely still because it is throbbing - I wish there were a word to express throbbing to the supreme degree of imperceptibility - with the Song, the Voice, of the Stillness. When that still, small Voice, infinitely potent by very reason of its small stillness, is heard, then are we hearing Kundalini - afar off, yes; inevitably so. But in the distant future to be our Voice, our very selves singing for joy.

So, too, in the perfect clarity of the silence, we shall

see a warmth because of its warmth of colour. Then shall we be seeing Kundalini - afar off, yes; inevitably so. But in the distant future to be our Colour, our very selves shining for joy.

ACCOUNT OF AN EXPERIENCE

CHAPTER 11

Let this little book conclude with an account of an experience which from one point of view may appear utterly remote from Kundalini, yet in fact was the direct result of the stimulation of this mighty Fire and of an apparent flowing on its surface " back" into the at present undiscoverable past. Indeed does Kundalini break down barriers, not merely of consciousness in terms of matter but no less in terms of time. The ridges between present and past, and present and future, become transcended, at all events within limits, and the Eternal becomes the Real rather than the modes of time. The student who was experimenting and experiencing was more interested in the past than in either present or future, so where travelling was possible he tended to travel " backwards" rather than outwards or forwards. Hence the experience which follows.

The student finds himself on a stream of Kundalini, and moves on the stream towards time's beginnings so far as this particular evolution is concerned.

He moves back and back and back, until he finds himself strangely immersed in the majestic profundities of the opening of a new era of life.

He looks about him, though who exactly this " he " is he does not know, largely because he does not care - it is that at which he is looking that absorbs him.

He sees before him - how entirely inadequate are descriptions which must needs be couched in small physical terminologies - a vast expanse of substance. Matter is not the right word at all, nor even is substance. The word Sea would be better if it did not so forcibly connote liquid. The sentence might well have read " a vast expanse of Fire," but there is inadequacy in this also.

At any rate there is a vast expanse, the nature of which is that it is known and therefore has within it the potentiality of knowing. Whether this sentence is intelligible or not is, perhaps, doubtful. But the dominant characteristic of the expanse is the fact that it is being known all the time, and that in such knowledge lies the fact of its own potency to know.

Being known, there is involved a Knower. And the student immediately conceives the principle that at the dawn of an evolutionary unfoldment there are two elements - a Known and a Knower. There is an infinitude of Known, and a Knower who in Himself sums up the apotheosis of the evolutionary process to which He belonged. He is a God and more than a God. He is a Sun.

The student perceives that by very reason of the Knower it might be postulated of the Known that it consists of an infinitude of Knowers in their becoming.

The Known comprises, therefore, innumerable Knowers who do not know.

Or, there are innumerable Fires which do not glow. On this expanse the Knower breathes the Fire of His knowing. And so evolution begins.

Innumerable Fires begin to glow in the spirit of their fireness, for the unconscious has met its mate in the conscious. The Known has met its mate in the Knower.

Sparks issue forth.

Sparks become microscopic flames.

And there is added the fuel of kingdom after kingdom of nature, fed by the Knower, who has known kingdoms and has brought them forth through the Fire of Kundalini.

The flames grow larger. More and more fuel-experience.

The flames burst into microscopic fires.

The fires expand into conflagrations - towering greatnesses of Fire.

Kingdom after kingdom feeds sparks and flames and fires, until all human fuel is resolved into Fire, as already has been the fuel of the mineral, vegetable and animal kingdoms before it.

And then Fires triumphant enter into the Essence of Fire. The very Form of Fire is consumed, and the Life of Fire shines forth in perfect purity.

From Fire-Form to Fire-Life.

Thus onwards into immeasurably transcendent regions, in which, perchance, even the Essence of Fire merges into that which lies beyond.

Thus from being Known, the Known becomes the Knower.

And the Knower withdraws into the transcendence of Being. On the bosom of Being He rests for re-creation.

THERE IS A HUSH OF THE SILENCE OF ETERNITY

In the Silence the clarion call of a pure Note of Forthgoing causing the Silence to vibrate in the rhythm of its own Perfection.

The Knower comes forth.

And on the expanse of a Known He breathes the Fire of his knowing.

Again begins an evolution.

And all are Knowers in the Becoming.

finis

AZILOTH BOOKS

Aziloth Books publishes a wide range of titles ranging from hard-to-find esoteric books - Parchment Books - to classic works on fiction, politics and philosophy - Cathedral Classics. Our newest venture is Aziloth Books Children's Classics, with vibrant new covers and Black-and-White/Colour illustrations to complement some of the world's very best children's tales. All our imprints are offered to the reader at a competitive price and through as many mediums and outlets as possible.

We are committed to excellent book production and strive, whenever possible, to add value to our titles with original images, maps and author introductions. With the premium on space in most modern dwellings, we also endeavour - within the limits of good book design - to make our products as slender as possible, allowing more books to be fitted into a given bookshelf area.

We are a small, approachable company and would love to hear any of your comments and suggestions on our plans, products, or indeed on absolutely anything. We look forward to meeting you.

Contact us at: info@azilothbooks.com.

PARCHMENT BOOKS enshrines the concept of the oneness of all true religious traditions - that "the light shines from many different lanterns". Our list below offers titles from both eastern and western spiritual traditions, including Christian, Judaic, Islamic, Daoist, Hindu and Buddhist mystical texts, as well as books on alchemy, hermeticism, paganism, etc..

By bringing together such spiritual texts, we hope to make esoteric and occult knowledge more readily available to those ready to receive it. We do not publish grimoires or any titles pertaining to the left hand path. Titles include:

Abandonment to Divine Providence	de Caussade
Corpus Hermeticum	G.R.S. Mead (trans.)
The Holy Rule of St Benedict	St. Benedict of Nursia
Kundalini	G. S. Arundale
The Way of Perfection	St. Teresa of Avila
Q.B.L.	Frater Achad
The Cloud Upon the Sanctuary	Eckhartshausen
The Confession of St Patrick	St. Patrick
Nightmare Tales; The Voice of the Silence	H. P. Blavatsky
The Outline of Sanity	G K Chesterton
The Teachings of Zoroaster	Shapuji A Kapadia
The Dialogue Of St Catherine Of Siena	St. Catherine of Siena
Esoteric Christianity	Annie Besant
The Wisdom of the Egyptians	Brian Brown
The Spiritual Exercises of St. Ignatius	St. Ignatius of Loyola
Moses and Monotheism	Sigmund Freud
Man, His True Nature & Ministry	St.-Martin
The Gospel of Thomas	Anonymous
The Imitation of Christ	Thomas à Kempis
The Interior Castle	St. Teresa of Avila
Songs of Innocence & Experience	William Blake
De Rerum Natura	Lucretius
The Secret of the Rosary	St. Louis de Montfort
Tertium Organum	P. D. Ouspensky
From Ritual to Romance	Jessie L. Weston
The God of the Witches	Margaret Murray
De Anima (Concerning the Soul)	Aristotle

Obtainable at all good online and local bookstores.
View Aziloth Books' full list at: www.azilothbooks.com

CATHEDRAL CLASSICS hosts an array of classic literature, from erudite ancient tomes to avant-garde, twentieth-century masterpieces, all of which deserve a place in your home. All the world's great novelists are here, Jane Austen, Dickens, Conrad, Arthur Machen and Henry James, brushing shoulders with such disparate luminaries as Sun Tzu, Marcus Aurelius, Kipling, Friedrich Nietzsche, Machiavelli, and Omar Khayam. A small selection is detailed below:

The Prophet	Kahlil Gibran
Herland; With Her in Ourland	CharlottePerkins Gilman
Frankenstein	Mary Shelley
The Time Machine; The Invisible Man	H. G. Wells
Three Men in a Boat	Jerome K Jerome
The Rubaiyat of Omar Khayyam	Omar Khayyam
A Study in Scarlet	Arthur Conan Doyle
Persuasion	Jane Austen
The Picture of Dorian Gray	Oscar Wilde
Flatland	Edwin A. Abbot
The Coming Race	Bulwer Lytton
The Adventures of Sherlock Holmes	Arthur Conan Doyle
The Great God Pan	Arthur Machen
Beyond Good and Evil	Friedrich Nietzsche
England, My England	D. H. Lawrence
The Castle of Otranto	Horace Walpole
Self-Reliance, & Other Essays (series1&2)	Ralph W. Emmerson
The Art of War	Sun Tzu
A Shepherd's Life	W. H. Hudson
The Double	Fyodor Dostoyevsky
To the Lighthouse; Mrs Dalloway	Virginia Woolf
The Sorrows of Young Werther	Johann W. Goethe
Leaves of Grass - 1855 edition	Walt Whitman
Analects	Confucius
Beowulf	Anonymous
Agnes Grey	Anne Bronte
Plain Tales From The Hills	Rudyard Kipling
The Subjection of Women	John Stuart Mill
The Rights of Man	Thomas Paine

Available at all good online and local bookstores.
View Aziloth Books' full list at: www.azilothbooks.com

THE CARTON CHRONICLES

THE CURIOUS TALE OF FLASHMAN'S TRUE FATHER

Keith Laidler

Morose, cynical and given to drink, Sydney Carton is one of Charles Dickens' most famous characters; a cold, dispassionate man, yet capable, in the final moments of A Tale of Two Cities, of sacrificing himself beneath the guillotine for Lucie, the woman he both loved and lost.

It now appears, however, that Dickens was being somewhat economical with the *actualité*.

Newly recovered documents, written in Carton's own hand, tell a far different tale. Sydney Carton survived his execution, only to find himself at the mercy of the monstrous Robespierre, author of the Paris Terror. His love Lucie languishes in a French prison, her husband dead, and Carton can ensure her survival only by becoming Robespierre's personal spy.

Reluctant, terrified and often drunk, Carton blunders his way through the major events of the French Revolution, grudgingly partaking in some of the blackest deeds of the Terror and, by a mixture of cowardice, bravado and luck, lending a hand in the fall of most of its leading figures. Kidnapped by the British, he finds himself a double agent, trusted by neither side. Our hero chronicles the slow decay of revolutionary ideals and, in passing, casts light on the true parentage of that sadistic villain of "Tom Brown's Schooldays", the beastly Flashman.

Praise for Keith Laidler's writing:

"Laidler's book is meticulously researched and covers a fascinating period" (The Times)

"It is a riveting story, and Laidler tells it well" (Telegraph Review)

From all good online and local bookstores.

www.ingramcontent.com/pod-product-compliance
Lightning Source LLC
Chambersburg PA
CBHW060135050426
42448CB00010B/2137